WOOD GREEN
THROUGH TIME
Albert Pinching

AMBERLEY PUBLISHING

First published 2013

Amberley Publishing
The Hill, Stroud, Gloucestershire, GL5 4EP
www.amberley-books.com

Copyright © Albert Pinching, 2013

The right of Albert Pinching to be identified as the
Author of this work has been asserted in accordance with
the Copyrights, Designs and Patents Act 1988.

ISBN 978 1 4456 1711 4 (print)
ISBN 978 1 4456 1720 6 (ebook)

British Library Cataloguing in Publication Data.
A catalogue record for this book is available from the
British Library.

Typesetting by Amberley Publishing.
Printed and bound in the UK by CPI Colour.

Introduction

Wood Green, situated 6 miles north of the City of London, is now part of the London Borough of Haringey. Although mainly residential, it is well known as a north London shopping centre, as well as for the iconic Alexandra Palace and Park.

In 1619, then part of the parish of Tottenham, it was a mere hamlet of ten houses on the periphery of Wood Green Common alongside the dominant Tottenham Wood, which later became the location of Alexandra Palace and Park. Its position close to the highway, once a droving road from London to Enfield and beyond, and later known as Green Lanes, encouraged its commercial development, starting with a smithy in 1770 and coaching inns from the late eighteenth century. By the end of the nineteenth century, the High Road was almost completely filled with shopping parades, and was completed at each end in the mid-1930s.

By 1844, it had a population of 400. Residential development was accelerated by the creation of the Great Northern Railway and the opening of its station at Wood Green (now Alexandra Palace station) in 1859, and by the Great Eastern Railway with its station at Palace Gates from 1878. Wood Green also became a hub for local transport with its depot for horse-drawn trams (from 1895), electric trams (from 1904), trolleybuses (1938) and diesel-powered buses (1961).

Wood Green became a parish of its own in 1866. It separated administratively from Tottenham in 1888, with a population of 23,000. It became an urban district in 1894, and a municipal borough in 1933, with a population of 54,000. It became part of the London Borough of Haringey in 1965.

Acknowledgements

I am indebted to the staff of Bruce Castle Museum (Haringey Archives & Local History Service) and my colleagues in the Hornsey Historical Society's Archives team for their assistance in the selection and provision of the majority of old images used in this book, the rest being from my own collection. With two exceptions, all new images are my own; the exceptions being the view of Barratts factory site (p. 55), for which I am indebted to Alan Griffiths, and to David Dell for the photograph of the portico of the Tottenham Wood farmhouse (p. 67). Also, I'd like to acknowledge L. R. Freeman/www.transporttreasury.co.uk for the use of the photograph of Palace Gates station (p. 77). I am most grateful to Mrs Christa Kenner Bedford for her permission to use her father's paintings of the Alexandra Palace and Park, made during the First World War, with credit to Collection IWM copyright artist's estate, which are held in the Imperial War Museum. I would also like to thank all my colleagues and friends for their encouragement during my undertaking of this work.

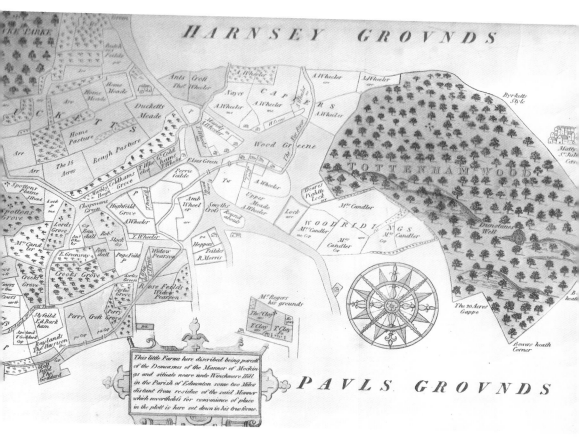

Tottenham Parish Plan, 1619

This was the first map to record Wood Green, and shows the common adjacent to Tottenham Wood traversed by the New River, which had been completed only six years earlier. The population of Wood Green at this time was around fifty. This map is known as the 'Upside Down Map', since for this map north is at the bottom. The Ordnance Survey map of 1920 (overleaf) shows the extent of development by that time, when the population was around 50,000. Since then, housing development has been mainly concentrated in the north-west corner of the area, known as Bounds Green.

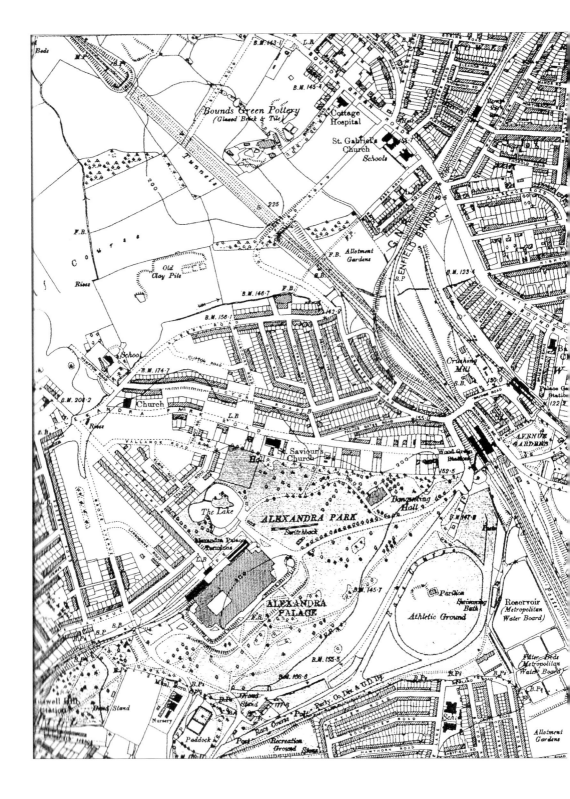

Corner of Lordship Lane and High Road, c. 1840

This unattributed and undated pen and ink sketch can be compared with a survey of 1844. The view looks south, approximately from the location of today's Wood Green Tube station. Chesser's forge is at left on what became known as Spouter's Corner. The pub sign (centre), which remained at that location well into the twentieth century, was for the Nag's Head Inn, which was one of the buildings on the right. The watery foreground is the original course of the New River. The current view features the red-fronted pub, The Goose (right), the late Victorian successor of the Nag's Head Inn. A single plane tree (left) still survives on the site of Spouter's Corner in front of a new Wetherspoon's pub of the same name.

Ducketts Farmhouse, High Road, *c.* 1840

Ducketts Farm, recorded from 1254, was located on the east side of the High Road, extending from Westbury Avenue in the south to Lordship Lane to the north. It became the location of the Noel Park Estate in the 1880s, when the moated farmhouse was replaced by Dovecote Avenue following the building of the shopping parades by the Artisans, Labourers & General Dwellings Co. Today, the now truncated Dovecote Avenue is a pedestrian precinct and location of market stalls, beyond which is the Sandlings housing development.

St Michael's Chapel of Ease, Junction of High Road and Bounds Green Road, 1850

Wood Green's first church, consecrated in 1844 and seating 250, was a chapel of ease in the parish of All Hallows, Tottenham. To meet the expanding population and to overcome problems of subsidence, the church was pulled down in 1865, with the exception of the chancel, and enlarged to accommodate 620. Later additions in 1874 included the tower, spire and a peal of six bells. The church later known as St Michael's and All Angels was Grade II listed. The tower, spire and other elevations were renovated in 2013.

Royal Masonic Institution Boys' School, Lordship Lane, c. 1860
The first Masonic Boys' School, accommodating seventy pupils, was opened in 1857 in Lordship Lodge, formerly a private house. This was replaced by the substantial Gothic building, accommodating 200 pupils and opened in 1865. The school moved to Bushey in Hertfordshire in 1898.

Wood Green Common, 1864

This view looks east over Wood Green Common from the slopes of the former Tottenham Wood Farm (now Alexandra Park) and shows the New River reservoir, created in 1859, in the middle distance. Beyond can be seen Moat Cottage (*c.* 1840) and, in the middle distance to the right, the first houses to be built in Mayes Road in 1863. The Great Northern Railway line, opened in 1850, runs across the view just beyond the reservoir. The present view from Alexandra Park shows the Wood Green Shopping City complex (centre) opened by HM Queen Elizabeth II in 1980. The white building in the centre foreground is the Heartlands High School, Wood Green's newest school, opened in 2011.

The New River, Near Myddleton Road, 1870

The New River was designed to bring fresh water from Chadwell Spring, near Ware in Hertfordshire, to London, following the 100-foot contour line. It was completed in 1613. To speed the flow, a large loop in the river through Wood Green and Tottenham was cut off by a tunnel between Myddleton Road and Station Road in 1859. Both ends of this tunnel have been Grade II listed by English Heritage. The painting was by C. Yardley. The recent view below is of the Station Road tunnel exit. Today, the New River Path follows the original route of the river through Wood Green.

The First Alexandra Palace, 1873

In 1863, the Alexandra Park Co. Ltd acquired the former Tottenham Wood Farm to establish a park and to build a 'Palace for the People', first proposed by Owen Jones in 1858. Alexandra Park opened in 1863, and horse racing began there in 1868. The first palace, designed by Alfred Meeson and offering a variety of entertainments, opened on 24 May 1873. It was destroyed by fire sixteen days later. These images are from the North Middlesex Photographic Society's collection, and are now held by the Hornsey Historical Society.

Westbury House, Off Earlham Grove, *c.* 1873

This large house was built around 1864/65, and became a family residence for Thomas William Smith Oakes, an East India merchant, from 1865–74. Later known as Earlham Grove House, it was occupied between 1876–86 by the philanthropic Smithies family. Mrs Catherine Smithies founded the Band of Mercy promoting animal welfare among young people; her son, Thomas, was a supporter of the working man and editor of *The British Workman*; both were vigorous campaigners for temperance. The house became Wood Green Town Hall in 1894, and the surrounding land became Town Hall Park, complete with a bowling green and bandstand.

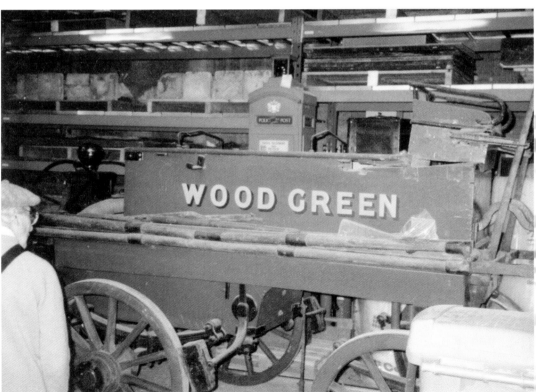

16

Wood Green's First Fire Station, Bounds Green Road, 1873

The watercolour (opposite above) by C. Yardley depicts the horse-drawn fire engine and the engine house, which was provided by the Tottenham Vestry in 1868 and operated by the Wood Green Volunteer Fire Brigade. It was located alongside St Michael's church. The engine still survives in the Museum of London's repository in Eagle Wharf Road, Islington. By 1901, a new engine house was erected alongside the Fishmongers Arms on the High Road. The original engine house later became a chapel of rest for a local undertaker. A purpose-built fire station with firemen's cottages adjacent was opened on the Bounds Green Road on 28 March 1914. The opening ceremony can be seen above.

Avenue Lodge, Bounds Green Road, 1879

In this 'animated' print, Avenue Lodge, on the corner of Park Avenue, is on the right, behind the animal drinking troughs. Built around 1870, it was a doctor's surgery before and after the turn of the twentieth century, home of the Wood Green Liberal Club in the 1920s and '30s, housed surveyors' and turf accountants' offices and a dancing school in the '50s and '60s, and was an MOT driving test centre during the '60s and '70s. In more recent times, it was home to various environmental groups and, most recently, the Greek Secondary School. It was refurbished in 2013, and continues to serve the community as a day nursery and pre-school.

The Three Jolly Butchers Hotel, 1889

Wood Green's first pubs were coaching inns, located on the High Road. This was the first, licensed in 1781 and situated on the hill that later took its name. Soon after this photograph was taken, it was transformed into a late Victorian hotel with much plate glass, a cupola and lanterns.

THREE JOLLY BUTCHERS HOTEL. H.A SPEECHLEY, PROPRIETOR. JOLLY BUTCHERS HILL, WOOD GREEN. N.

The Nags Head Inn, High Road, 1889
Wood Green's second coaching inn was established around 1840 and located opposite Spouter's Corner. It underwent a late Victorian makeover around 1900, and the external features of the Victorian building remain today. It was renamed The Goose and Granite in the 1990s, and is now known as The Goose.

Chitts Hill House, *c.* 1890

This fine Regency house was built around 1800 and stood among 48 acres of grounds. It occupied the high ground just north of today's Woodside Park, with the New River flowing on its east and west flanks. It was the family home of Quaker banker John Overend (1769–1832) and his wife Mary (1783–1862), who was a noted benefactor to Tottenham. The Overends were succeeded by the family of Samuel Page (1810–86), until 1881. Samuel Page made generous benefactions to the parish church of St Michael, including its tower, spire and peal of six bells in 1874. Today, the only survivor of the Chitts Hill Estate is the Grade II-listed former gatehouse or lodge (built 1822), now located in the corner of Woodside Park. It is Wood Green's oldest surviving building. It became refreshment rooms in the days of Town Hall Park and a children's playhouse (known then as The Mushroom House) in the 1970s, after which it was in private residential use for a short time in the 1990s.

Nightingale Hall, Bounds Green Road, 1890

This substantial building was part of an estate extending from the Bounds Green Road to the Albert Road Recreation Ground, originally known as Woodreddings, carved from the eastern flank of the Tottenham Wood in the fifteenth century (see 1619 Tottenham Plan on page 5). It became a farm and was bisected by the Great Northern Railway in 1850, the western half being added to the adjacent Tottenham Wood Farm. The 10-acre eastern part of the estate was sold in 1890, and the North London Cycling and Athletic Grounds was established on the site where the Wood Green Cycling Track operated from 1895 to 1900. In addition to cycling, Wild West shows (presented by the showman and pioneer aviator Colonel W. F. Cody), football and other events were held here. The 1896 photograph shows the start of a race in front of the main grandstand. The former grounds later became the location of Braemar, Cornwall and Northcott Avenues in the early years of the twentieth century.

Wood Green Cycling Track, Bounds Green Road, 1896
Another view of the cycling track, looking west, shows a 24-hour professional race in progress. The second open grandstand is seen at right, behind which can be seen the towers of Palace Gates railway station. The modern view is of Braemar Avenue, laid out in 1903–07, which effectively replaced the back straight.

Wood Green Police Station, High Road, 1898 Wood Green's first purpose-built police station on the corner of Nightingale Road was opened in 1866. It was enlarged and given an Edwardian façade in 1908. The building was further enlarged in 2013, but retains the Edwardian façade.

The Alexandra Park Tavern, High Road, 1899

This tavern, dating from 1870, with its adjacent tea gardens, stood on the east side of the High Road, close to the corner of Lymington Avenue and opposite Mayes Road. By the turn of the twentieth century, the ground floor of the pub had been extended and the tea gardens replaced with shops. Today, the site is dominated by the eastern side of the Shopping City.

St James' Presbyterian Church, Corner of Canning Crescent and High Road, *c.* 1900

The church was built in 1878, and replaced an iron-clad building. In 1903, its Sunday attendances were among the highest Presbyterian figures in London. The congregation united with the Bowes Park congregational church in the 1950s, after which the building became a warehouse. It was demolished in the late 1970s to make way for the present housing.

The Printers' Almshouses, Bounds Green Road, *c.* 1900

These almshouses, originally accommodating twelve couples, were opened in 1856. It was extended in 1871 to house twenty-four couples, and further extended in 1891. It was closed in 1969, and the residents were transferred to Bushey in Hertfordshire. The almshouses were demolished in 1970, and replaced in 1974 by Greenriding House, a telecommunications switching centre.

St Michael-at-Bowes Church, Corner of Palmerston Road and Whittington Road, *c.* 1900
This view is from the south-west, with the New River in the foreground. The church was designed by Sir George Gilbert Scott, and consecrated in 1874. It was the first mission church to be established in the original parish of St Michael's, Wood Green. As a result of the ravages of damp, cold and dry rot over the years, the church was demolished in 1986. A new church with an integrated hall was built on the site and consecrated in 1988.

Snakes Lane, 1902

This rural byway from Lordship Lane to White Hart Lane, with Elm Lodge Farm to its left, survived until the beginning of the twentieth century. By 1914, the farmland had become the Scotch Estate, and Snakes Lane became Perth Road. The southern part of Perth Road still retains a green character by virtue of Chapmans Green (right) at the corner of Lordship Lane.

Station Road, *c.* 1903

This view looks west from the High Road. The weatherboarded shop, the adjacent Elm Cottages and the original Jolly Anglers pub beyond were recorded in 1837. The current view shows a plethora of new office buildings, shops and flats, but the remodelled Jolly Anglers pub of 1904 remains in the middle distance. The railway bridge in the far distance was removed after closure of the Palace Gates line in 1963.

Corner of High Road and Turnpike Lane, 1905

At the left is the Wellington pub, dating from around 1870, with a horse-drawn omnibus waiting outside. Electric trams run along the High Road. On the right, the upper floors of the then surviving Dovecote Villas can be seen above the shops. The terraced houses beyond the pub (left) were demolished in the mid-1930s to make way for a new shopping parade, which was dominated by Montague Burton's tailor's store with Art Deco Native American imagery on its white façade, and a temperance billiard hall on the first floor. By the 1990s, the Wellington had become a Burger King restaurant and the pub was reduced to a bar next door in Turnpike Lane. Most recently, Burger King has been replaced by a Costa Coffee establishment.

Home & Colonial Society's Training College for School Mistresses, Lordship Lane, 1904
This college was opened in 1904 and occupied the former Masonic Boys' School building. It remained until 1930, when the building became the headquarters of the Tottenham District Gas Board. A dormitory group of students, dated 1922, is shown below.

Jolly Butchers' Hill, 1904 and 1960s

The hill in the far distance from Spouter's Corner (right) to St Michael's church, once named Church Hill, takes its popular name from the former coaching inn on its west side, The Three Jolly Butchers. To the left are Gladstone Gardens, behind which stood a detached house, The Elms. The tramlines in the foreground were for horse-drawn trams; a depot was located on the west side of the hill from 1895. The depot was converted for electric trams in 1904, and overhead wires soon became part of the scene. In 1938, trolleybuses were introduced and the depot again converted. The comparable view from the 1960s shows several Routemaster diesel-powered buses, introduced from 1958.

Top of Jolly Butchers' Hill, 1904 and 2013
This view from the corner of High Road and Bounds Green Road (left) shows the Printers' Almshouses (far left) and St Michael's church (right). The recent view shows the telecommunications switching centre, which replaced the almshouses in the 1970s, and the church tower and spire looking pristine after renovation in 2013.

St Paul's Roman Catholic Church, Station Road, 1905 and 2013

The Roman Catholic parish of St Paul the Apostle was created in 1882. The first church (above right) was a 'tin tabernacle' erected in the same year. The larger church in Romanesque style, designed by E. Goldie, was consecrated in 1904, the earlier building becoming the church hall. Both were replaced by a new building, designed by John Rochford in 1970. Stained glass from the second church features in the corridor of the present church. St Paul's Catholic Primary School is located on Bradley Road at the rear of the church.

Wood Green Congregational Church, Lordship Lane, c. 1905
Wood Green's first nonconformist church opened in 1864, and was operational for 100 years before amalgamating with the Harringay congregational church. It then became the Haringey Arts Centre in the 1960s, and in its declining years was a cheap furniture store. Demolished in 2005, despite local campaigns to retain it for community use, it has been replaced by a block of flats with a gymnasium on the ground floor.

Fishmongers' and Poulterers' Almshouses, High Road, c. 1905

These almshouses, opened in 1849, were the first of several to move out of the crowded City of London to Wood Green during the nineteenth century. Accommodating twelve married couples, they survived until 1955, when they were demolished to make way for the Wood Green Civic Centre, which opened in 1958. It became the Haringey Civic Centre in 1965 after the creation of the London Borough of Haringey, which comprised the former municipal boroughs of Hornsey, Tottenham and Wood Green.

United Charities of St Leonard's, Shoreditch Almshouses, Nightingale Road, *c.* 1905
These almshouses originated in Shoreditch. John Fuller's Almshouses, dating from 1605, came to Wood Green in 1866, and were rebuilt by the United Charities in 1904, along with St Leonard's House (façade below) and the Porter's and Walter's Almshouses. The original foundation stone from Shoreditch is located in the grounds. All these buildings, and the iron gates and railings, were Grade II listed and remain today. More recent accommodation has been built in the adjacent Truro Road.

The Nightingale Hotel, High Road, *c.* 1905
Located on the corner of Nightingale Road, the Nightingale Hotel was originally the Nightingale Tavern, dating from 1866, with an adjacent Masonic Hall. It was known as 'The Bird' by the Wood Green Cycling Track fraternity. By 2000, it had been reduced to a single-storey building, and was demolished in 2004. The site is now occupied by a block of flats.

Wood Green Railway Station, 1905
The Great Northern Railway from London to York, created in 1850, opened its station at Wood Green in 1859. This view looking south shows the footbridge linking the booking offices on both sides of the tracks with the platforms. In 1873, after the opening of Alexandra Palace, the station was renamed Wood Green (Alexandra Park), reverting to Wood Green in 1971. The recent view shows the present station, named Alexandra Palace since 1982, now part of First Capital Connect's Great Northern Route, with upgrades providing new platforms in 2013.

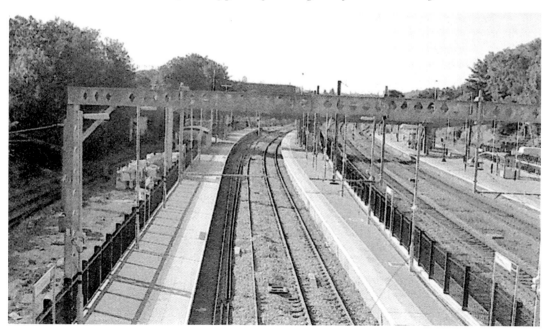

The Three Jolly Butchers Hotel, 1910
The above view presents the late Victorian splendour of the hotel exterior with plate glass and lanterns. Below, a contemporary view of the opulent interior.

Obelisk, Bounds Green Road, *c.* 1900

This 21-foot-high granite obelisk with adjacent drinking troughs was erected in 1879 by public subscription in the middle of the Bounds Green Road, at the junction with Park Avenue, to commemorate the life and work of Mrs Catherine Smithies (1785–1877), a tireless campaigner for animal welfare and temperance, who lived at Earlham Grove House. In 1904, the obelisk had to be moved to make way for the laying of rails for the North Metropolitan Tramways. It was moved to its present position on the grass verge, ironically facing the The Prince (formerly The Prince of Wales) public house.

Gladstone Terrace, High Road, *c.* 1910

This view is from Gladstone Gardens, looking towards Noel Park railway station. The shopping parade (left) between Gladstone Road and the railway bridge was completed in 1886, as part of the Noel Park Estate Development by the Artisans, Labourers & General Dwellings Company. It was the first purpose-built parade on the High Road. Gladstone Gardens (right) were replaced in the 1930s by the Broadway Parade. The present view shows little change to the shopping parade, but the railway station and bridge have been replaced by the Shopping City.

Wood Green Baptist Chapel, Finsbury Road, c. 1910
This chapel was built in 1875 and seated 200. A larger church, seating 500 and designed by George Baines, was built on the corner of nearby Braemar Avenue and opened in 1907. The original chapel was then occupied by the Catholic Apostolic church from 1906–65, and then became the Greek Orthodox church of St Barnabas, which it remains today.

The Kings Arms Hotel, Corner of High Road and White Hart Lane, _c._ 1905
This large establishment with adjacent assembly hall dates from 1870 and was a popular venue for many local events. It underwent several name changes in recent years, such as The Kings (around the 1990s) and Charley Browns (around 2000). The assembly rooms were converted to become the Grand Palace Banqueting Suite in 2005, with a Polish bar on the ground floor and the N22 nightclub occupying the former stables area at the rear.

Trinity Wesleyan Chapel, Trinity Road, *c.* 1910
This chapel, dedicated in 1872, was the first of fifty Wesleyan Methodist chapels to be established in the London area, funded by Sir Francis Lycett MP. In 1903, it had the largest Sunday attendances of all nonconformist churches in the area. It became the Greek Orthodox Cathedral of St Mary in 1970. Seriously damaged by fire in the 1980s, it was rebuilt in sympathy with the original building, and continues to serve the Greek Orthodox community of north London today.

Jolly Butchers' Hill, *c.* **1900 and 1910**
The upper view features a horse-drawn tram and the ornate lanterns of the Nags Head pub, the sign can of which be seen opposite on Spouter's Corner. The lower view shows an electric tram, introduced in 1905, with associated wirescape. The shops on the right, on the corner of Lordship Lane, became the location of Wood Green Underground station in 1932.

HIGH ROAD WOOD GREEN

St Gabriel's Church, Bounds Green, 1910

Bounds Green was once a hamlet 1 mile north-west of Wood Green. The upper view from Brownlow Road shows its first mission church (left). It was originally St Peter's, built in 1883, and later became St Gabriel's. In 1906, a new, larger church of St Gabriel's (centre) was built on the corner of Durnsford Road on the creation of the new parish. The original church became the parish hall until its demolition in 1934. St Gabriel's was declared redundant and demolished in 1983. The site was developed for housing with the semi-circular Madison Apartments on the site of the church and St Gabriel's Court beyond, both dating from 2006. Plans to build a new church on the site did not materialise.

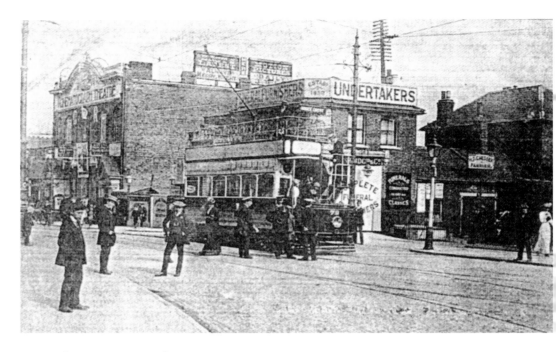

Spouter's Corner, 1913 and 2000
This view of the corner of Lordship Lane and the High Road shows Chesser's forge (right), dating from 1770, and Burridge's undertakers, established in 1850, who occupied the site until the 1970s. Further left is the Cinematograph Theatre, opened in 1910, one of Wood Green's early cinemas. It later became a furniture depository, with a dance school on the first floor. In the 1980s, the building became the indoor Market Hall, adjacent to the Wood Green open-air market. Between 1997 and 2000, the whole corner was transformed into its present form, the Hollywood Green, the location of a multi-screen cinema, shops and restaurants.

The Triangle, Crescent Road, *c.* 1910 and 2013

This early view looks towards the junction with Palace Gates Road (left). The parade of shops on the right are dated 1898, being one of Wood Green's early local shopping parades. The paved triangle at the road junction in the distance was once the location of a polling booth at election times. Today, the triangle is the location of the summer fête of the Palace Gates Residents Association, who also tend the plantings on the site.

Spouter's Corner, 1921 and 2000
This watercolour of Chesser's forge, by J. E. Savery, is dated 1921. The forge was established in 1770, being the first commercial enterprise on the High Road. Today, Spouter's Corner is known as Hollywood Green, an entertainment complex (see page 50).

Cheapside Parade, High Road, *c.* 1920 and 2013

This view looks south from the corner of Mayes Road. On the left, the Edmonds Bros department store dominates the corner of Lymington Avenue. Also on the left is the Cheapside Parade, another part of the Noel Park Estate development. The turrets at each end were completed in 1912, and the Wood Green Empire theatre was its centerpiece, with its prominent cupola. The Cheapside Parade replaced three pairs of large villas, built in the 1860s, along the east side of the High Road. The No. 29 bus (centre) ran along the High Road from 1911. The recent view shows little change, except that the southern end of the Shopping City now dominates the corner of Lymington Avenue, and the former theatre building has lost its cupola. The shops on the west side of the High Road (right) have changed little, except for the nature of the businesses. The No. 29 diesel bus, among others, still plies this route.

Alexandra Park Nursing Home, Alexandra Park Road, *c.* 1920
Established as a private nursing home, it was used for the rehabilitation and care of military casualties during the First World War, and was the Alexandra Maternity Home from 1940 until 1972. The site was redeveloped in the later 1970s, and is now occupied by Hilldene Court, providing sheltered housing and retirement flats.

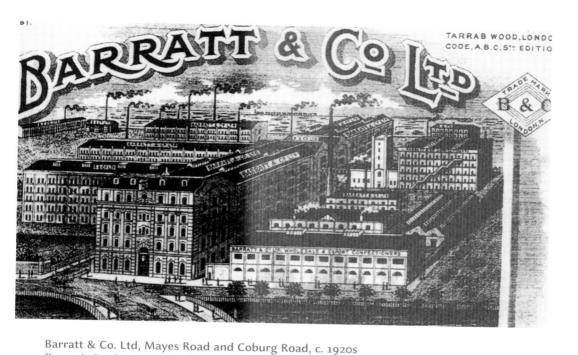

Barratt & Co. Ltd, Mayes Road and Coburg Road, c. 1920s

Barratt's Confectionery Works, an important Wood Green institution, was established in a former piano factory in Mayes Road in 1880. New buildings were added in 1904, 1922, 1924 and 1952. The somewhat exaggerated letterhead view of the factory site (above) was dated 1927. Barratt's was Wood Green's largest employer, and their wide range of products were world famous. It became part of the Bassett Group in 1966, the Wood Green site closed in 1980, and the plant transferred to Sheffield. The view below is of the former Barratt's factory site in 1997, with its prominent office in Mayes Road at right. The curved, white-fronted building (left) dates from 1922 and is located in Coburg Road. It is now a clothing factory. The Alexandra Palace overlooks the scene from its lofty position in the distance.

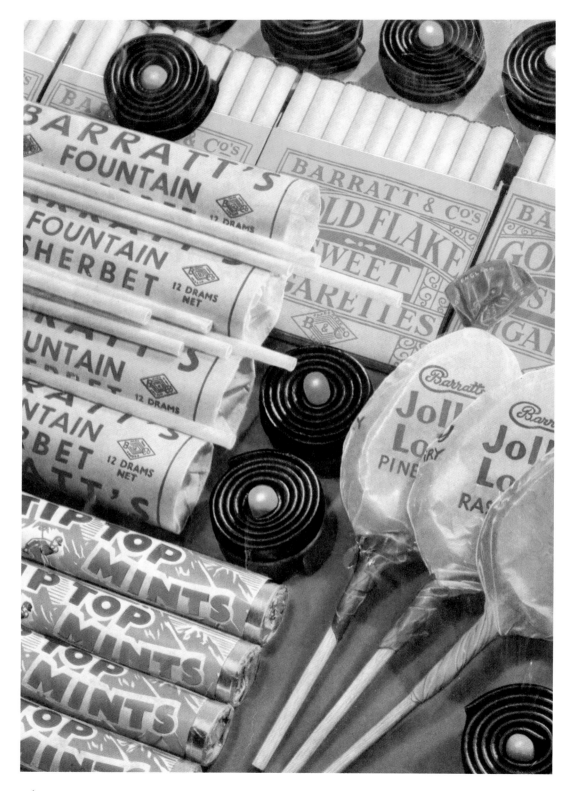

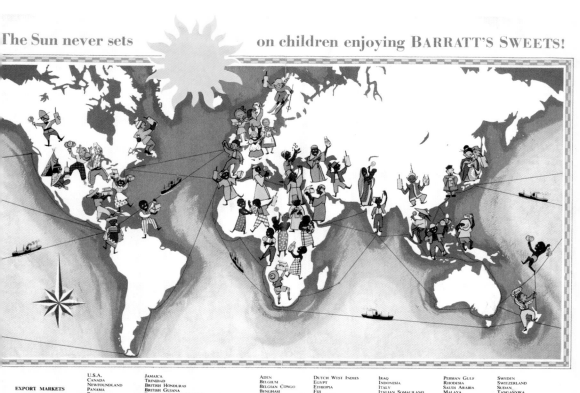

EXPORT MARKETS

U.S.A.	JAMAICA	ADEN	DUTCH WEST INDIES	IRAQ	PERSIAN GULF	SWEDEN
CANADA	TRINIDAD	BELGIUM	EGYPT	INDONESIA	RHODESIA	SWITZERLAND
NEWFOUNDLAND	BRITISH HONDURAS	BELGIAN CONGO	ETHIOPIA	ITALY	SAUDI ARABIA	SUDAN
PANAMA	BRITISH GUIANA	BENGHASI	FIJI	ITALIAN SOMALILAND	MALAYA	TANGANYIKA
BERMUDA	ECUADOR, SOUTH AMERICA	CYPRUS	GIBRALTER	KENYA	NEW ZEALAND	TRIPOLITANIA
BARBADOS	N.A.A.F.I. (HAMBURG & PARIS)	CASABLANCA	HELIGOLAND	LEBANON	PORTUGAL	THAILAND
BAHAMAS	U.S. ARMY (GERMANY, TRIESTE & GREECE)	CEYLON	HONG KONG	MALTA	PAKISTAN	WEST AFRICA

Barratt & Co. Ltd Advertisement
On the opposite page can be seen an assortment of sweet goods produced by Barratt's. Above, a map depicting children from across the globe enjoying Barratt's sweets.

War Memorial, Crescent Gardens, High Road, 1920 and 1999

Above, the unveiling of this memorial in Portland stone, raised by public subscription, took place on 11 November 1920. It commemorated the 982 Wood Green residents who fell in the First World War. A further 254 names of the service personnel who perished in the Second World War were added and dedicated on 9 November 1947.

St Saviour's Church, Alexandra Park Road, Early 1920s
This church, designed by J. S. Alder, was consecrated in 1909, replacing an iron-clad church of 1900. The war memorial (left) was dedicated to parishioners who fell in the First World War. The church closed in 1993, and was demolished and replaced by a private housing development in 1998. Today, the war memorial stands in the forecourt of the St Saviour's Court housing complex, and is the focus of a local annual Remembrance Service.

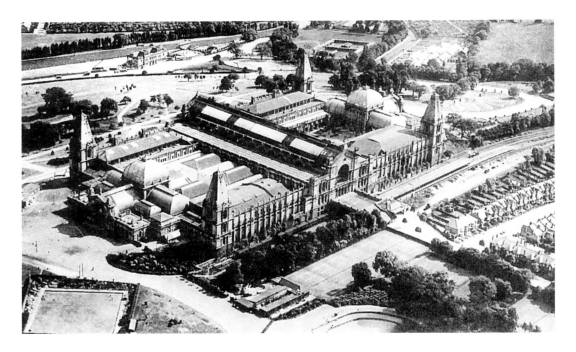

The Second Alexandra Palace, 1928

This aerial view from the north-east is of the second Alexandra Palace, opened in 1875. The railway line from Finsbury Park terminated on the north side of the palace. The bowling green can be seen at bottom left, and the racecourse grandstand is just left of top centre, and the lake close to bottom right. In 1935, the BBC installed its television transmission mast on the south-east corner turret, and television broadcasting began on 2 November 1936. In 1980, the palace was again the subject of another fire, resulting in serious damage to the great hall and the western end of the building. After major restoration work, the palace was reopened in 1988, and remains an iconic feature on the north London skyline and venue for exhibitions, and musical and sporting events.

Wood Green Town Hall, *c.* 1920

The extension to the town hall (right) was added in 1913 to house the council chamber and a magistrates' court. After the opening of the Wood Green Civic Centre in 1958, the former town hall was renamed Woodside House, catering for the elderly and special needs services of Wood Green and, subsequently, Haringey Council, which it remains today. The surrounding land is now Woodside Park. Today, many external features of the mid-Victorian house remain, except for the loss of its prominent chimney stacks.

Great Eastern Railway Bridge, High Road, 1910
The Great Eastern Railway branch line from Seven Sisters to Palace Gates crossed the High Road just north of today's Shopping City. The former elevated Noel Park station is seen at right. The railway closed in 1963 under Dr Beeching's axe, releasing the land to make way for the building of the Shopping City. Today, a new bridge, or walkway, linking the east and west parts of the Shopping City is located a few metres south of the former railway bridge.

Passmore Edwards Cottage Hospital, Bounds Green Road, c. 1910
This hospital, funded by the Passmore Edwards Foundation, was opened in 1895 and had eight beds. It was enlarged to fifty-two beds in 1922, and additional facilities had been added by 1927. Taking patients from Hornsey, Southgate and Wood Green, it was later known as Wood Green Cottage Hospital. It came under NHS administration in 1948, and under the local health authority in 1974. It closed in 1985. The site is now occupied by Passmore Edwards House, which provides sheltered accommodation, and the adjacent Bounds Green Health Centre.

High Road, *c.* 1950s and 2013

This view looks southwards from Spouter's Corner. At right is the Broadway Parade, with the then Odeon cinema at its centre. On the left is the Gladstone Terrace shopping parade. In the distance is the bridge that carried what was then the LNER railway across the High Road. The recent view is almost identical, except that in the distance is the red-brick edifice of the Shopping City, with its walkway across the High Road. The white building on the left, on the corner of Gladstone Avenue, was originally a branch of the National Provincial Bank and, more recently, a Vietnamese restaurant. Currently, it is a Coffee Republic outlet.

The Elms, High Road, *c.* 1900
This detached house, built around
1860, stood in its own grounds on the
west side of the High Road, fronted
by Gladstone Gardens, opposite
Spouter's Corner. It was demolished
in the mid-1930s to make way for the
Broadway Parade. The central feature
of the Broadway was the Gaumont
Palace Cinema, built in 1934 in lavish
Art Deco style, with seating for 2,556,
and a 170-seat restaurant. In 1962, it
was renamed The Odeon, underwent
refurbishment in 1967, and was 'tripled'
in 1973. It closed as a cinema in 1984
and was converted, retaining many
of its original features, to a Top Rank
Bingo Club, which subsequently closed.
The building was Grade II listed in
1990. It was closed between 1996 and
2000, except for a functions suite and
nightclub, which occupied the former
restaurant area. The building was then
Grade II* listed in 2000. In 2004, it
became the Dominion Centre, operated
by the UPG ministries as a community
church and Christian bookshop. A
nightclub still operates on the first floor.

Durnsford Road Lido, *c.* **1935**

One of the first actions of the newly incorporated Wood Green Borough Council in 1933 was to build an Olympic-size open-air swimming pool or lido on the Albert Road Recreation Ground in Durnsford Road. It was duly opened in 1934, becoming Wood Green's third swimming pool at that time. It was a popular venue for over fifty years, before closing in 1989 and being converted into the Sunshine Garden Centre, now also a popular venue, which reflects the change in leisure pursuits over the years.

Tottenham Wood House, Rhodes Avenue, *c. 1930*
This farmhouse at Tottenham Wood farm dates from around 1800 and became the clubhouse of the Muswell Hill Golf Club from 1894–1931. Today only the portico remains, located within a small copse at the corner of Rhodes Avenue and Albert Road.

Bounds Green Road, _c._ 1900

This view looks east towards St Michael's church. Carthorses wait their turn at the water trough at the corner of Finsbury Road. In the centre distance is the Higher Grade Board School, opened in 1899. At left, beyond Trinity Gardens, is the Trinity Wesleyan chapel in Trinity Road. The obelisk, commemorating the life and work of Mrs Catherine Smithies, was transferred to the other side of the road in 1904 to make way for the installation of electric tram rails.

The Fishmongers Arms, High Road, *c.* 1906

This was the first large roadside tavern in Wood Green. It dates from 1853 and was located on the corner with Trinity Road. To the right of the pub is Wood Green's second fire station, opened in 1901. The Bourne Hall to the rear of the pub in Trinity Road was a popular venue for meetings, and home of the Wood Green Jazz Club in the 1950s and '60s. In the 1990s, it was renamed O'Rafferty's Irish Pub. It was refurbished in 2007 with the upper floors converted to flats. Currently, the ground floor serves as a local neighbourhood police front office. The Bourne Hall was demolished in 2009 and replaced by a terrace of five small houses.

Dovecote Villas, High Road, 1905

Twelve pairs of three-storey villas (right) with large front gardens extended from today's Lymington Avenue to Whymark Avenue. They were built in 1862, on the Ducketts farmland, fronting the east side of the High Road (or Green Lanes, as it was then known). Some of these villas were to give way to the Artisans, Labourers & General Dwellings Co. development of Cheapside Parade by 1912. The villas further south were replaced by Barton's department store in the 1920s. The Barton's 1960s building is shown below, and was in turn replaced by the present Marks & Spencer and BHS stores. Shops were initially built over the front gardens of the villas, and some upper floors of the villas can be seen behind the stores.

Wood Green Public Library, 1908

The library was a gift of the Andrew Carnegie Foundation. It stood on the corner of the High Road and Station Road and was opened in September 1907. With its red-facing dome and clock, it remained a local landmark until the office building boom of the 1970s, when it was replaced by the tinted glass-fronted River Park House, currently occupied by council offices.

Brabançonne Villa, High Road, *c.* 1930

This elegant mid-Victorian villa (built in 1870) stood at the corner of the High Road and Earlham Grove in an acre of grounds. For fifty years (1871–1920), it was the home of Colonel Arthur Durrant JP (1839–99), a local Liberal politician and dignatory, and his family. In 1921, the house and grounds were purchased by the Daughters of Providence, a Catholic teaching order, for use as the senior school for their Providence Convent School for girls, which had been established in Wood Green in 1905 and initially occupied houses in Bounds Green Road and Stuart Crescent. In 1926, a new purpose-built St Angela's Providence High School was erected on the site of the orchard at the rear of the villa. In the same year, the villa itself became the Providence Convent for the sisters. In 1934, the school amalgamated with another convent school in nearby Palmers Green, with the senior schools remaining in Wood Green. The convent also relocated to Palmers Green, the villa being sold in 1938. With the outbreak of the Second World War, the school pupils were evacuated and the villa and the school building occupied by the ARP and the Army Medical Corps. A British restaurant was also housed in the school building during the war. After the war, the school building returned to its normal use. Later, the villa was in commercial use and sold to Wood Green Council in 1955. It was demolished by Haringey Council in the 1970s to make way for municipal flats. The school building became the Cypriot Community Centre in the 1970s, which it remains today, having been refurbished after a fire in 2003.

Lordship Lane, Wood Green.

Corner, Lordship Lane and High Road, 1920/1997
This view looks east along Lordship Lane with a parade of shops (left) opposite Spouter's Corner (right). In 1932, these shops were replaced by the Wood Green Underground station as part of the Piccadilly line extension from Finsbury Park to Cockfosters.

Woodall House, Lordship Lane, 1930

The Tottenham & District Gas Co. purchased the Home & Colonial Training College and its grounds in 1930, renaming it Woodall House after its chairman. It later became the offices of Eastern Gas. In 1974, Haringey Council purchased the site, of which 10 acres were used for housing. Woodall House was renovated and remodelled to become Wood Green Crown Court, which opened in 1989.

Ranelagh House, Bounds Green, 1930

This detached family house, dating from the early 1870s, stood in an acre of grounds on the corner of the Bounds Green Road and Brownlow Road. It was demolished in 1931 to make way for the building of Bounds Green Undergound station, opened in 1932 as part of the Piccadilly line extension from Finsbury Park to Cockfosters. The station was the victim of a severe bombing incident in October 1940. A high explosive bomb destroyed two adjacent houses and the blast penetrated down to the platforms below, then in use as emergency air-raid shelters. There were twenty-two fatalities and many injuries. The station was Grade II listed in 2010.

High Road, Wood Green

High Road, *c.* 1960 and 2013

The earlier view shows Barton's department store dominating the east side of the High Road. This building replaced a colonnaded building of the 1920s. The 1960s building was seriously damaged by fire and not rebuilt. Today, this section of the High Road has an uninspiring appearance, incorporating a large BHS store and smaller shops.

Palace Gates Railway Station, c. 1960

The Alexandra Park branch line of the Great Eastern Railway, going from Seven Sisters and terminating at Palace Gates, was opened in 1878. The upper view of the station, taken just before its closure, shows the frontage on the footpath between Braemar Avenue and Cornwall Avenue. Another entrance, connected by a covered footbridge, and the goods entrance were located in Dorset Road on the other (western) side of the tracks. The line was closed in 1963, and the station demolished to make way for a design award-winning sheltered and family housing development, completed in 1986.

Palace Gates Railway Station, *c.* 1965
This rather forlorn view of the western and goods entrance to the station at the corner of Bridge Road and Dorset Road was taken soon after the closure of the LNER (formerly Great Eastern) Seven Sisters to Palace Gates branch line in 1963. Today, the site is the location of a residential close, with access from Dorset Road.

Palace Gates Railway Station, 1968
This view of the eastern entrance on the footpath between Braemar and Cornwall Avenues was taken after its closure. The view today shows part of the housing development that replaced the station.

Wood Green Common Recreation Ground, 2004 and 2013
This recreation ground, with its distinctive red-brick wall on its western boundary, was laid out in 1908. It is a surviving 6-acre remnant of the original Wood Green Common. Its eastern boundary is flanked by mature plane trees. The recent view shows the Heartlands High School, Haringey's newest secondary school, opened in 2011 and occupying land between the boundary wall and the main line railway. For some years previously, this land had been a permanent Travellers' site.

Cambridge House, Mayes Road, 1997
This imposing building was the Barratt & Co. Confectioners head office and dates from 1887. It is now occupied by the Metropolitan Housing Trust and other enterprises. After Barratt's departure from Wood Green in 1980, some of its former buildings were incorporated in the Wood Green Business Centre and, in the 1990s, others became part of The Chocolate Factory, a collection of cultural and artistic enterprises.

Finsbury Road, 1997 and 2013
The first residential development in Wood Green began in the 1860s, between the High Road and Bounds Green Road to the north of St Michael's church. Finsbury Road was one of its first shopping streets, with thirty shops by 1884. The upper view shows the remaining southern section with a few surviving shops and cottages, and the spire of the former Baptist chapel in the distance. The later view shows most of the shops converted to residential properties. The corner shop was formerly King Bros ironmongers and hardware merchants, at No. 51. They were established in 1884, and were in business here for over 100 years.

Bowes Park Congregational Church, c. 1912

Bowes Park congregational church was registered in 1902, with a hall and classrooms on the corner of Arcadian Gardens and the High Road. The large, adjacent red-brick church was registered in 1912. In 1950, the congregation joined with St James Presbyterian church, to become the United Reformed church of St James-at-Bowes. Since the 1980s, the building has served the congregation of the New Testament Church of God.

Myddleton Road, Bowes Park, 1905

The Bowes Park district of Wood Green, on the former Bowes Manor Estate, grew around Bowes Park station after it was opened in 1880. Myddleton Road was its principal shopping street, starting with four shops in 1884, forty in 1984 and eighty in 1912, and included many major provisions stores. By the 1970s, competition from the High Road and later the Shopping City reduced the number of retail shops, and a number have been converted to residential use. Today, the upper elevations of the street are largely unchanged and many of the shops are now in non-retail use.

Jolly Butchers' Hill, *c.* 1910 and 2013

Looking south from the corner of Watsons Road. On the right is the turreted entrance to the electric tram depot, Cakebread, Robey & Co., builders merchants, and the dome of the Wood Green Central Library on the corner of Station Road, beyond which can be seen the façade of the Nag's Head pub. On the left is the parade of shops once known as Hardy Terrace. In the modern view is the entrance to the bus depot and the frontage of River Park House, which replaced the library in the 1970s. On the left, the large, flat-fronted building (with scaffolding) is a London Transport services building. It dates from 1932 and was part of the Piccadilly Line tube extension facilities.

New Fire Tender, 1919

Wood Green's first motorised fire tender outside the Bounds Green Road Fire Station. The local fire service subsequently became part of the Middlesex Fire and Ambulance Service, and integrated with the London Fire Brigade. Following rationalisation, the fire station became redundant, but the building remains today as the Bounds Green Ambulance Station.

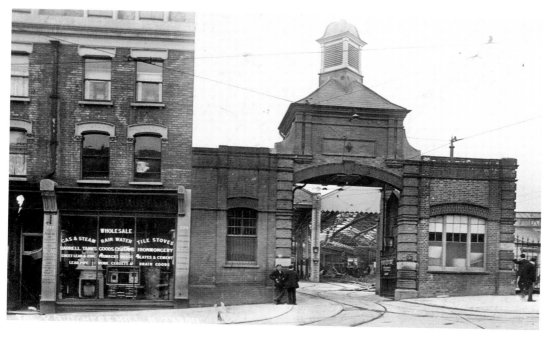

Wood Green Tram Depot, High Road, *c.* 1910

This depot on the west side of Jolly Butchers' Hill was opened by the Metropolitan Tramways and Omnibus Co. Ltd in 1895, for horse-drawn trams and stabling. By 1904, the depot had been transferred to Metropolitan Electric Tramways, and converted to accommodate sixty-two electric trams. By 1938, the depot was again converted to accommodate over 100 trolleybuses. In 1961, trolleybuses were replaced by diesel-powered buses, and the depot was again modified. Currently, the depot is operated by Arriva for London Transport. The depot, now known as Wood Green Bus Garage, remains an important hub in the local transport network.

Higher Gade School, Bounds Green Road, *c*.1905

This school, located between Bounds Green Road and Trinity Road, was Wood Green's first secondary school and opened in 1899. In 1924, it became Trinity County School, which later moved to the former Wood Green County School building (built in 1910) in Glendale Avenue, overlooking Woodside Park. Following the various educational changes of the '60s and '70s, the Glendale Avenue building (below) became the home of the St Thomas More Roman Catholic coeducational school in 1967, which it remains today. The Bounds Green Road building housed the Nightingale Primary School until recently. It is now the Trinity Primary Academy and has changed little externally.

Alexandra Palace and Park During the First World War, 1914–18

On 8 August 1914, Alexandra Palace and Park was closed to the public 'until further notice'. During 1914/15, the palace served as a temporary home for Belgian civilian refugees displaced from their homeland following the German invasion of Belgium. In all, 38,000 refugees passed through the palace during this period. In 1915, the palace and part of the park became an internment camp for enemy aliens, accommodating up to 3,000 internees, mainly German and Austrian civilians. One of these, George Kenner, was an artist who made a unique series of paintings that recorded everyday scenes during his time there in 1915/16, displayed on the next few pages. Some of these paintings record parts of the palace and park later lost in the redevelopment following the fire of 1980. The scenes include the roller skating rink, in use as sleeping quarters; a wintry landscape in the Italian Gardens; internees on the south slope, with a unique view of the racecourse grandstand and a sentry post; and the theatre in use for a service. The palace and park were restored to normal use in 1920.

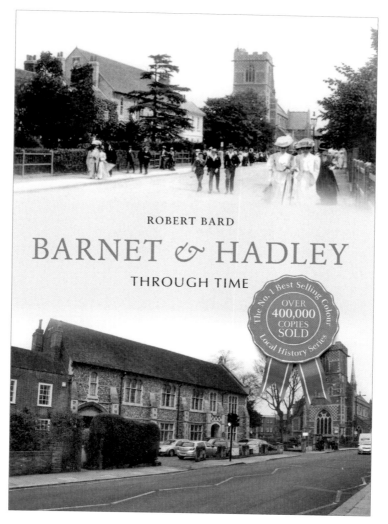

Life in 1940s London
Mike Hutton

With the help of people who lived through the traumatic times
of the 1940s, Mike Hutton vividly recreates the atmosphere of a
London that is so far removed from the one of today.

978 1 4456 0826 6
224 pages

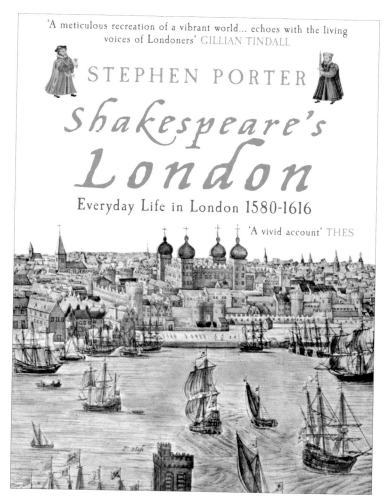

'A meticulous recreation of a vibrant world... echoes with the living voices of Londoners' GILLIAN TINDALL

STEPHEN PORTER

Shakespeare's London

Everyday Life in London 1580-1616

'A vivid account' THES

Shakespeare's London
Stephen Porter

Shakespeare's London was a bustling, teeming metropolis that was growing so rapidly the government took repeated, and ineffectual, steps to curb its expansion. From contemporary letters, journals and diaries, Stephen Porter creates a vivid picture of this fascinating city, with its many opportunities and also its persistent problems.

978 1 84868 200 9
96 pages, full colour

Available from all good bookshops or order direct
from our website www.amberleybooks.com

Lost London in Colour

Brian Girling

This fascinating compilation of early London photographs takes us
on a tour of one of the world's greatest cities, the historic scenes,
dating back to the 1850s, reproduced in full colour.

978 1 4456 1502 8
128 pages, full colour